2020...A year that will live in infamy. For our family, it was a year we stopped down, smelled the roses, cleaned out our closets, learned to bake banana bread, and in my case, I began a ritual that lasted for 52 weeks called #ThrowItBackThursday. What started as a fun way to signify that we survived another week of pandemic lockdown, turned into a humorous discovery and exploration of cocktails from around the world. Each cocktail became an expression of the insanity and challenges we all faced while trapped with kids and dogs in our suburban home.

Key lessons learned from the pandemic.... You can never have enough toilet paper...You definitely need yeast to bake.... And most importantly, always keep a well-stocked bar.

We hope you enjoy "THE LOST YEAR, an epic journey of discovery by a family that faced down a pandemic with humor and mixed drinks!"

L'chaim,

Josh Lawson

A special thanks to my wife for putting up with my weekly bartending sessions, although she got to enjoy all of them! Thanks to my girls, my boys and my parents and in-laws (beaming with pride). Thank you also to TAZ for the amazing book design, to Kevin McGinnis for the beautiful photography and to the "bubble" drinking crew, Juliet, Jeff and Gigi.

WEEK 1
MOSCOW MULE

2 OZ. GREY GOOSE VODKA
½ OZ. FRESH SQUEEZED LIME JUICE
4 TO 6 OZ. BUNDABERG GINGER BEER
1 LIME WHEEL - GARNISH

SQUEEZE LIME JUICE INTO A MOSCOW MULE COPPER MUG. ADD CRUSHED ICE HALF AND THEN POUR IN THE VODKA. FILL THE REST WITH COLD GINGER BEER, STIR, ADD LIME WHEEL AND SERVE.

WEEK 2
OLD FASHIONED

2 OZ. BULLEIT RYE WHISKEY
2-3 DASHES OF AUSTRALIAN
BITTERS COMPANY
1 SUGAR CUBE OR ½ OZ. SIMPLE SYRUP
1 ORANGE TWIST - GARNISH

PUT SUGAR CUBE IN LOWBALL GLASS. COVER THE CUBE WITH 2-3 DASHES OF BITTERS. ADD WHISKEY AND STIR UNTIL SUGAR CUBE DIS-SOLVES. ADD ICE (SINGLE LARGE CUBE IF AVAILABLE), STIR AGAIN AND THEN GARNISH WITH ORANGE TWIST AND SERVE.

WEEK 3
APEROL SPRITZ

APEROL
LAMARCA PROSECCO
CLUB SODA
1 ORANGE SLICE - GARNISH

FILL A WINE GLASS HALF WAY WITH ICE AND THEN POUR HALF THE GLASS FULL OF APEROL. POUR EQUAL AMOUNT OF PROSECCO. ADD A SPLASH OF CLUB SODA, GENTLY STIR AND GARNISH WITH A SLICE OF ORANGE.

WEEK 4
MOJITO

2 OZ. CAPTAIN MORGAN WHITE RUM
½ OZ. SIMPLE SYRUP
¾ OZ. FRESH SQUEEZED LIME JUICE
CLUB SODA
3 MINT LEAVES

USING A COCKTAIL SHAKER, GENTLY MUDDLE THE 3 MINT LEAVES AND THEN ADD ICE, RUM, SIMPLE SYRUP AND LIME JUICE. SHAKE TO CHILL AND STRAIN INTO A HIGHBALL GLASS WITH CRUSHED ICE. TOP WITH CLUB SODA, GENTLY STIR AND GARNISH WITH A MINT SPRIG.

WEEK 5
MARGARITA

2 OZ. CASAMIGOS TEQUILA BLANCO
1 OZ. COINTREAU
1 OZ. FRESH SQUEEZED LIME JUICE
1 LIME WHEEL - GARNISH
SALT FOR THE RIM (IF PREFERRED)

USING A COCKTAIL SHAKER, ADD THE TEQUILA, COINTREAU AND LIME JUICE, ADDING A SMALL AMOUNT OF ICE. SHAKE TO CHILL AND POUR INTO A LOWBALL GLASS FILLED WITH ICE AND GARNISH WITH A LIME WHEEL. IF SALTED RIM IS PREFERRED, SALT PRIOR TO POURING.

WEEK 6
FRENCH 75

2 OZ. TANQUERAY GIN
2 DASHES SIMPLE SYRUP
½ OZ. LEMON JUICE OR FRESH SQUEEZED LEMON JUICE (PREFERRED)
KORBEL CHAMPAGNE

USING A COCKTAIL SHAKER, ADD THE GIN, SIMPLE SYRUP AND LEMON JUICE OVER ICE. SHAKE TO CHILL AND STRAIN INTO A CHAMPAGNE FLUTE. TOP WITH CHAMPAGNE.

WEEK 7
NEGRONI

1 OZ. BOMBAY SAPPHIRE GIN
1 OZ. CAMPARI
1 OZ. MARTINI & ROSSI SWEET VERMOUTH
ORANGE TWIST - GARNISH

POUR GIN, CAMPARI AND VERMOUTH IN A
LOWBALL GLASS WITH ICE. STIR AND GARNISH
WITH THE ORANGE TWIST.

WEEK 8
VODKA GIMLET

1 OZ. GREY GOOSE VODKA
¾ OZ. SIMPLE SYRUP
¾ OZ. FRESH SQUEEZED LIME JUICE
LIME WHEEL - GARNISH

USING A COCKTAIL SHAKER, ADD THE VODKA,
SIMPLE SYRUP, LIME JUICE AND ICE. SHAKE
TILL CHILLED AND STRAIN INTO A LOWBALL
OR COUPE GLASS. GARNISH WITH LIME
WHEEL.

4

WEEK 9
DARK & STORMY

**1 ½ OZ. THE KRAKEN BLACK SPICED RUM
BUNDABERG GINGER BEER**

FILL A HIGHBALL GLASS WITH ICE, ADDING
RUM AND TOPPING IT OFF WITH COLD
GINGER BEER. GARNISH WITH LIME WHEEL.

WEEK 10
PALOMA

**2 OZ. CASAMIGOS TEQUILA BLANCO
½ OZ. FRESH SQUEEZED LIME JUICE
SQUIRT OR GRAPEFRUIT SODA
LIME WHEEL - GARNISH
GRAPEFRUIT SLICE - GARNISH
SALT FOR THE RIM (IF PREFERRED)**

ADD TEQUILA AND LIME JUICE TO AN ICE
FILLED GLASS (SALT THE RIM PRIOR, IF
PREFERRED). TOP WITH GRAPEFRUIT SODA
AND GARNISH WITH LIME WHEEL AND SLICE
OF GRAPEFRUIT.

WEEK 11
CAIPIRINHA

2 OZ. LEBLON CACHAÇA
1 WHOLE LIME, CUT INTO WEDGES
2 TSP. SUGAR
LIME WHEEL - GARNISH

PLACE LIME WEDGES INTO A LOWBALL
GLASS. POUR SUGAR AND MUDDLE LIMES
TILL THEY HAVE DISSOLVED THE SUGAR
INTO THE LIME JUICE. ADD CACHAÇA AND
STIR. ADD CRUSHED ICE AND LIME WHEEL
FOR GARNISH.

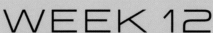

WEEK 12
CORN 'N' OIL

2 OZ. THE KRAKEN BLACK SPICED RUM
½ OZ. JOHN D. TAYLOR'S VELVET FALERNUM
½ OZ. FRESH SQUEEZED LIME JUICE
3 DASHES OF AUSTRALIAN BITTERS
COMPANY
LIME WEDGE - GARNISH

FILL A LOWBALL GLASS WITH ICE. ADD THE
VELVET FALERNUM AND THEN TOP WITH THE
RUM, FOLLOWED BY THE LIME JUICE ON TOP.
DASH THE BITTERS ON TOP OF THE LIME JUICE
AND STIR TO COMBINE. GARNISH WITH THE
LIME WHEEL.

WEEK 13
PIMM'S CUP

1 ¾ OZ. PIMM'S NO. 1
5 OZ. GINGER ALE OR LEMONADE
ORANGE SLICES
STRAWBERRY SLICES
CUCUMBER SLICES
MINT SPRIG - GARNISH

FILL A HIGHBALL GLASS WITH THE ORANGE, STRAWBERRY AND CUCUMBER SLICES, ADDING ICE AS YOU GO. POUR PIMM'S NO. 1 AND THEN TOP WITH GINGER ALE OR LEMONADE. STIR AND GARNISH WITH MINT SPRIG.

WEEK 14
CADILLAC MARGARITA

1 ½ OZ. CASA AZUL REPOSADO
1 OZ. GRAND MARNIER
¾ OZ. FRESH SQUEEZED LIME JUICE
1 LIME WHEEL - GARNISH
SALT FOR THE RIM (IF PREFERRED)

USING A COCKTAIL SHAKER, ADD THE TEQUILA, GRAND MARNIER AND LIME JUICE, ADDING A SMALL AMOUNT OF ICE. SHAKE TO CHILL AND POUR INTO A LOWBALL GLASS FILLED WITH ICE AND GARNISH WITH A LIME WHEEL. IF SALTED RIM IS PREFERRED, SALT PRIOR TO POURING.

WEEK 15
CHERUB'S CUP

2 OZ. GREY GOOSE VODKA
1 OZ. ST. GERMAIN ELDERFLOWER LIQUEUR
3 OZ. KORBEL BRUT ROSÉ
¼ OZ. SIMPLE SYRUP
¾ OZ. FRESH SQUEEZED LEMON JUICE
1 STRAWBERRY
STRAWBERRY - GARNISH

USING A COCKTAIL SHAKER, ADD THE
STRAWBERRY, LEMON JUICE, AND SIMPLE SYRUP
AND MUDDLE. ONCE MUDDLED, ADD ICE, THE ST.
GERMAIN AND VODKA. SHAKE TILL CHILLED.
STRAIN OVER FRESH ICE IN A COLLINS
GLASS. TOP WITH BRUT ROSÉ AND
GARNISH WITH STRAWBERRY.

WEEK 16
FRENCH PEAR MARTINI

1 ½ OZ. WILD ROOTS PEAR INFUSED VODKA
1 ½ OZ. ST. GERMAIN ELDERFLOWER LIQUEUR
1 OZ. KORBEL BRUT CHAMPAGNE
SUPERFINE SUGAR - FOR RIM
PEAR SLICE - GARNISH

USING A COCKTAIL SHAKER, FILL WITH ICE AND
ADD ST. GERMAIN AND PEAR VODKA. SHAKE WELL
TILL CHILLED AND STRAIN INTO THE PREPARED
MARTINI GLASS (CAN ADD SUPERFINE SUGAR TO
RIM PRIOR USING A LEMON OR LIME WEDGE TO
WET THE RIM OF THE GLASS, ROLLING THE RIM IN
THE SUGAR). GARNISH WITH PEAR SLICE.

WEEK 17
OLD CUBAN

1 ½ OZ. CAPTAIN MORGAN WHITE RUM
2 OZ. KORBEL BRUT CHAMPAGNE
1 OZ. SIMPLE SYRUP
¾ FRESH SQUEEZED LIME JUICE
2 DASHES OF AUSTRALIAN BITTERS COMPANY
6 WHOLE MINT LEAVES
1 MINT SPRIG - GARNISH

USING A COCKTAIL SHAKER, MUDDLE THE MINT LEAVES WITH THE SIMPLE SYRUP AND LIME JUICE. ADD THE RUM, THE DASH OF BITTERS AND ICE. SHAKE WELL TILL CHILLED AND THEN DOUBLE STRAIN INTO A COUPE GLASS. TOP WITH CHAMPAGNE AND GARNISH WITH THE MINT SPRIG.

WEEK 18
TOM COLLINS

2 OZ. AVIATION AMERICAN GIN
1 OZ. FRESH SQUEEZED LEMON JUICE
½ OZ. SIMPLE SYRUP
CLUB SODA
LEMON PEEL - GARNISH

USING A COLLINS GLASS, ADD THE GIN, LEMON JUICE AND SIMPLE SYRUP. ADD ICE AND TO WITH CLUB SODA. STIR GENTLY AND THEN GARNISH WITH THE LEMON PEEL.

WEEK 19
COSMOPOLITAN

**1 ½ OZ. GREY GOOSE VODKA
(OR CITRUS VODKA)
1 OZ. COINTREAU
½ OZ. FRESH SQUEEZED LIME JUICE
¼ OZ. CRANBERRY JUICE
(IN THIS INSTANCE CRAN-STRAWBERRY)
LEMON PEEL OR LIME WHEEL - GARNISH**

USING A COCKTAIL SHAKER, POUR VODKA,
COINTREAU, LIME JUICE AND CRANBERRY
JUICE. ADD ICE AND SHAKE WELL TILL
CHILLED. STRAIN INTO A MARTINI GLASS AND
GARNISH WITH LEMON PEEL OR LIME WHEEL.

WEEK 20
PB WHISKEY ROOT BEER

**1 ½ OZ. SKREWBALL PEANUT BUTTER WHISKEY
½ OZ. BAILEY'S IRISH CREAM LIQUEUR
3 OZ. IBC ROOT BEER**

USING A COLLINS GLASS OR SODA MUG, ADD
ICE AND THEN POUR IN WHISKEY AND BAI-
LEY'S. TOP WITH ROOT BEER.

WEEK 21
JUNGLE BIRD

1 ½ OZ. THE KRAKEN BLACK SPICED RUM
¾ OZ. CAMPARI
1 ½ OZ. PINEAPPLE JUICE
½ OZ. FRESH SQUEEZED LIME JUICE
½ OZ. SIMPLE SYRUP (OR DEMERARA SYRUP)
PINEAPPLE WEDGE - GARNISH

USING A COCKTAIL SHAKER, ADD THE RUM, CAMPARI, PINEAPPLE JUICE, LIME JUICE AND SIMPLE SYRUP (OR DEMERARA SYRUP). ADD ICE AND SHAKE UNTIL WELL CHILLED. STRAIN INTO A LOWBALL GLASS OVER FRESH ICE. GARNISH WITH A PINEAPPLE WEDGE.

WEEK 22
GIN GIN MULE

1 ½ OZ. TANQUERAY GIN
1 OZ. SIMPLE SYRUP
4-5 OZ. BUNDABERG GINGER BEER
¾ OZ. FRESH SQUEEZED LIME JUICE
8 MINT LEAVES
MINT SPRIG - GARNISH

USING A COCKTAIL SHAKER, ADD THE MINT LEAVES, LIME JUICE AND SIMPLE SYRUP. MUDDLE WELL TO RELEASE THE MINT ESSENCE. ADD GIN AND FILL THE SHAKER WITH ICE. SHAKE WELL TILL CHILLED AND THEN STRAIN INTO A HIGHBALL GLASS WITH FRESH ICE. TOP WITH GINGER BEER AND GARNISH WITH THE MINT SPRIG.

WEEK 23

STRAWBERRY MOJITO

2 OZ. CAPTAIN MORGAN'S WHITE RUM
1 OZ. SIMPLE SYRUP
½ OZ. FRESH SQUEEZED LIME JUICE
6 MINT LEAVES
4 STRAWBERRIES
CLUB SODA
MINT SPRIG & STRAWBERRY - GARNISH

USING A HIGHBALL GLASS, ADD STRAWBERRIES, MINT LEAVES, SIMPLE SYRUP AND LIME JUICE. MUDDLE WELL TO RELEASE MINT ESSENCE AND BREAK DOWN STRAWBERRIES. ADD CRUSHED ICE AND RUM. TOP WITH CLUB SODA AND STIR WELL. GARNISH WITH MINT SPRIG AND STRAWBERRY.

WEEK 24

SCOTCH ON THE ROCK

2-3 OZ. THE BALVENIE DOUBLE WOOD 12 YEAR SINGLE MALT SCOTCH WHISKEY

USING A LOWBALL GLASS, ADD A SINGLE LARGE CUBE OR ROUND BALL OF ICE. POUR SCOTCH.

WEEK 25
BLUE LAGOON

1 OZ. GREY GOOSE VODKA
1 OZ. DEKUYPER BLUE CURAÇAO
4 OZ. LEMONADE
LEMON WHEEL - GARNISH

USING A COCKTAIL SHAKER, ADD THE VODKA, CURAÇAO AND LEMONADE. ADD ICE AND SHAKE UNTIL WELL CHILLED. STRAIN INTO A HIGHBALL GLASS (OR HURRICANE GLASS) WITH FRESH ICE AND GARNISH WITH THE LEMON WHEEL.

WEEK 26
GEORGIA PEACH

1 OZ. GREY GOOSE VODKA
2 OZ. DEKUYPER PEACHTREE SCHNAPPS
4 OZ. LEMONADE
¼ OZ. ROSE'S GRENADINE

USING A COCKTAIL SHAKER, ADD THE VODKA, SCHNAPPS, LEMONADE AND GRENADINE. SHAKE WELL TILL CHILLED. POUR INTO A LOWBALL GLASS OVER FRESH ICE.

WEEK 27

THE MADRAS

1 ½ OZ. GREY GOOSE VODKA
3 OZ. CRANBERRY JUICE
1 OZ. ORANGE JUICE
LIME WEDGE - GARNISH

USING A HIGHBALL GLASS, POUR THE VODKA, CRANBERRY JUICE AND ORANGE JUICE OVER ICE. STIR WELL AND GARNISH WITH LIME WEDGE.

WEEK 28

PINEAPPLE MEZCAL MARGARITA

2 OZ. YOLA 1971 MEZCAL
1 OZ. CASAMIGOS TEQUILA BLANCO
1 OZ. GRAND MARNIER
1 OZ. FRESH SQUEEZED LIME JUICE
½ OZ. BLUE AGAVE NECTAR
4 OZ. PINEAPPLE JUICE
SALT FOR THE RIM - GARNISH
PINEAPPLE WEDGE - GARNISH

USING A COCKTAIL SHAKER, ADD THE MEZCAL, TEQUILA, GRAND MARNIER, LIME JUICE, BLUE AGAVE AND PINEAPPLE JUICE OVER ICE. SHAKE WELL TILL CHILLED. POUR INTO A LOWBALL GLASS AND GARNISH WITH PINEAPPLE WEDGE. IF SALTED RIM IS PREFERRED, SALT PRIOR TO POURING.

WEEK 29
MAI TAI

1 ½ OZ. CAPTAIN MORGAN'S WHITE RUM
¾ OZ. THE KRAKEN BLACK SPICED RUM
½ OZ. DEKUYPER ORANGE CURAÇAO
½ OZ. TRADER VIC'S ORGEAT ALMOND SYRUP
½ OZ. FRESH SQUEEZED LIME JUICE
LIME WHEEL - GARNISH
MINT SPRIG - GARNISH

USING A COCKTAIL SHAKER, ADD THE WHITE RUM, CURAÇAO, LIME JUICE, ORGEAT SYRUP OVER CRUSHED ICE AND SHAKE GENTLY FOR 3 SECONDS. STRAIN INTO A LOWBALL GLASS OVER CRUSHED ICE AND FLOAT THE DARK RUM ON TOP. GARNISH WITH A LIME WHEEL AND MINT SPRIG.

WEEK 30
SIDECAR

2 OZ. HENNESSY VS COGNAC
1 OZ. COINTREAU
¾ OZ. FRESH SQUEEZED LEMON JUICE
SUGAR - FOR THE RIM OF THE GLASS

USING A COCKTAIL SHAKER, ADD THE COGNAC, COINTREAU AND LEMON JUICE. ADD ICE AND SHAKE WELL TILL CHILLED. STRAIN INTO A MARTINI GLASS WITH A SUGAR COATED RIM.

WEEK 31

THE MAN O' WAR

2 OZ. FOUR ROSES SMALL BATCH
 SELECT BOURBON
1 OZ. COINTREAU
½ OZ. NOILLY PRAT SWEET VERMOUTH
½ OZ. FRESH SQUEEZED LEMON JUICE
LEMON PEEL - GARNISH

USING A COCKTAIL SHAKER, ADD THE BOURBON,
COINTREAU, SWEET VERMOUTH AND LEMON JUICE
OVER ICE. SHAKE WELL TILL CHILLED. STRAIN INTO
A LOWBALL GLASS FILLED WITH CRUSHED ICE.
GARNISH WITH A LEMON PEEL.

WEEK 32

BOURBON LEMONADE

1.5OZ. BULLEIT BOURBON
4 OZ. LEMONADE
LEMON SLICE - GARNISH

USING A HIGHBALL GLASS, ADD THE
BOURBON AND LEMONADE ON TOP OF ICE.
STIR WELL AND GARNISH WITH A LEMON
SLICE.

16

WEEK 33
GIN FIZZ

2 OZ. BOMBAY SAPPHIRE GIN
¾ OZ. FRESH SQUEEZED LEMON JUICE
½ OZ. SIMPLE SYRUP
1 EGG WHITE (OPTIONAL)
SODA WATER
LEMON TWIST - GARNISH

USING A COCKTAIL SHAKER, ADD THE GIN, LEMON JUICE, SIMPLE SYRUP AND EGG WHITE. SHAKE VIGOROUSLY FOR 15 SECONDS. FILL THE COCKTAIL SHAKER WITH ICE AND SHAKE WELL TILL CHILLED. STRAIN INTO A LOWBALL GLASS AND TOP WITH SODA WATER. GARNISH WITH A LEMON TWIST.

WEEK 34
THE CILLA

2 ½ OZ. CASAMIGOS REPOSADO TEQUILA
½ OZ. BLUE AGAVE NECTAR
½ OZ. FRESH SQUEEZED LIME
SODA WATER
LIME WEDGE - GARNISH

USING A COCKTAIL SHAKER, ADD THE TEQUILA, AGAVE AND LIME JUICE. ADD ICE AND SHAKE TILL WELL CHILLED. POUR INTO A LOWBALL GLASS WITH ICE AND TOP WITH SODA WATER. ADD LIME WEDGE FOR GARNISH.

WEEK 35
PINK LADY

1 ½ OZ. BOMBAY SAPPHIRE GIN
¾ OZ. LAIRD'S APPLEJACK BRANDY
¼ OZ. FRESH SQUEEZED LEMON JUICE
2 DASHES GRENADINE
1 EGG WHITE
CHERRY - GARNISH

USING A COCKTAIL SHAKER FILLED WITH ICE, ADD
THE GIN, BRANDY, LEMON JUICE AND EGG WHITE.
SHAKE VIGOROUSLY UNTIL WELL CHILLED. STRAIN
INTO A CHILLED COUPE OR MARTINI GLASS AND
GARNISH WITH CHERRY.

WEEK 36
EL GUAPO

2 OZ. CASAMIGOS BLANCO TEQUILA
½ OZ. DESERT PEAR SYRUP
¾ OZ. FRESH SQUEEZED LIME JUICE
BUNDABERG GINGER BEER
LIME WEDGE - GARNISH

USING A COCKTAIL SHAKER FILLED WITH ICE,
ADD THE TEQUILA, PEAR SYRUP AND LIME
JUICE. SHAKE VIGOROUSLY UNTIL WELL
CHILLED. POUR INTO A LOWBALL GLASS WITH
FRESH ICE AND THEN ADD GINGER BEER TO
THE TOP. GARNISH WITH LIME WEDGE.

WEEK 37
SAKEN' IT TO ME

2 ½ OZ. TYKU SAKE
1 OZ. ST. GERMAIN
½ OZ. FRESH SQUEEZED LEMON JUICE
2 DASHES ANGOSTURA CITRUS BITTERS
1 OZ. POMEGRANATE JUICE
KORBEL BRUT CHAMPAGNE
LEMON TWIST - GARNISH

USING A COCKTAIL SHAKER FILLED WITH ICE, ADD THE SAKE, ST. GERMAIN, LEMON JUICE, CITRUS BITTERS AND POMEGRANATE JUICE. SHAKE WELL TILL CHILLED AND THEN STRAIN INTO A CHAMPAGNE FLUTE. TOP WITH CHAMPAGNE AND GARNISH WITH A LEMON TWIST.

WEEK 38
THANKSGIVING RUM PUNCH

1 GALLON HONEYCRISP APPLE CIDER
2 CUPS ORANGE JUICE
2 CUPS KRAKEN BLACK SPICED RUM
2-3 HONEYCRISP APPLES SLICED
1-2 ORANGES SLICED
2-3 CINNAMON STICKS
APPLE SLICES - GARNISH
ORANGE SLICES - GARNISH

COMBINE ALL INGREDIENTS INTO A LARGE PUNCH BOWL OR LARGE PITCHER. REFRIGERATE FOR 1-2 HOURS PRIOR TO SERVING. USE SLICED APPLE AND ORANGES AS GARNISH.

WEEK 39

ELDERFLOWER ROSE GIMLET

2 OZ. BOMBAY SAPPHIRE GIN
1 ½ OZ. ST. GERMAIN
1 ½ OZ. FRESH SQUEEZED LIME JUICE
½ OZ. SIMPLE SYRUP
½ TEASPOON ROSE WATER
ROSE PETALS - GARNISH

USING A COCKTAIL SHAKER FILLED WITH ICE, ADD THE GIN, ST. GERMAIN, LIME JUICE, SIMPLE SYRUP AND ROSE WATER. SHAKE WELL TILL CHILLED. POUR INTO A LOWBALL GLASS FILLED WITH ICE. GARNISH WITH ROSE PETALS.

WEEK 40

APPLE PIE

3 OZ. FOUR ROSES SMALL BATCH SELECT BOURBON
2 OZ. HONEY SYRUP
1 DROP VANILLA EXTRACT
MARTINELLI'S SPARKLING APPLE CIDER
APPLE ROUND - GARNISH
CINNAMON STICK - GARNISH

USING A COCKTAIL SHAKER FILLED WITH ICE, ADD THE BOURBON, HONEY SYRUP AND VANILLA EXTRACT. SHAKE WELL TILL CHILLED. POUR INTO A HIGHBALL GLASS FILLED WITH ICE AND ADD MARTINELLI'S SPARKLING APPLE CIDER. GARNISH WITH APPLE ROUND AND/OR CINNAMON STICK.

WEEK 41
LAWSON LIBATION

1 OZ. KRAKEN BLACK SPICED RUM
¼ OZ. MEZCAL UNION
¼ OZ. LISMORE SINGLE MALT SCOTCH WHISKY
¼ OZ. SIMPLE SYRUP
½ OZ. FRESH SQUEEZED LIME JUICE
1 DASH OF COCA-COLA
LIME WEDGE - GARNISH

USING A ROCKS GLASS WITH ICE, ADD DARK RUM, MEZCAL, SCOTCH WHISKY, SIMPLE SYRUP, FRESH SQUEEZED LIME JUICE AND THE DASH OF CO-CA-COLA. STIR TILL CHILLED AND GARNISH WITH LIME WEDGE.

WEEK 42
PORNSTAR

1 ½ OZ. STOLI VANILLA VODKA
½ OZ. GIFFARD FRUIT DE LA PASSION LIQUER
1 OZ. PASSION FRUIT PUREE
½ OZ. FRESH SQUEEZED LIME JUICE
½ OZ. VANILLA SIMPLE SYRUP
2 OZ. LAMARCA PROSECCO
PASSION FRUIT SLICE - GARNISH

USING A COCKTAIL SHAKER FILLED WITH ICE, ADD THE VODKA, GIFFARD FRUIT DE LA PASSION LIQUER, PASSION FRUIT PUREE, FRESH SQUEEZED LIME JUICE AND VANILLA SIMPLE SYRUP. SHAKE WELL TILL CHILLED. STRAIN INTO A WELL-CHILLED COUPE GLASS. SERVE WITH A SHOT GLASS SIDE OF LAMARCA PROSECCO.

WEEK 43
TEQUILA OASIS

1 ½ OZ. CASAMIGOS TEQUILA BLANCO
½ OZ. TRIPLE SEC
¾ OZ. FRESH SQUEEZED LIME JUICE
3 OZ. PINEAPPLE JUICE
LIME WEDGE - GARNISH

USING A COCKTAIL SHAKER FILLED WITH ICE, ADD
THE TEQUILA, TRIPLE SEC, FRESH SQUEEZED LIME
JUICE AND PINEAPPLE JUICE. SHAKE TILL WELL
CHILLED, POUR INTO A COLLINS GLASS AND
GARNISH WITH A LIME WEDGE.

WEEK 44
PEACH ME

2 ½ OZ. WOODFORD RESERVE BOURBON
½ OZ. DEKUYPER PEACHTREE SCHNAPPS
1 LUXARDO MARASCHINO CHERRY
1 ORANGE SLICE
3 DASHES ANGOSTURA ORANGE BITTERS
ORANGE SLICE - GARNISH

USING A COCKTAIL SHAKER, MUDDLE THE
CHERRY, ORANGE SLICE AND BITTERS. ADD
THE BOURBON AND ICE AND STIR TILL WELL
CHILLED. STRAIN INTO A ROCKS GLASS OVER
A LARGE CUBE AND GARNISH WITH THE
ORANGE SLICE.

WEEK 45
PURPLE HAZE

1 ½ OZ. GREY GOOSE VODKA
½ OZ. CHAMBORD LIQUEUR
2 OZ. CRANBERRY JUICE
GINGER ALE
MINT SPRIG - GARNISH
BLACKBERRIES - GARNISH

USING A COCKTAIL SHAKER WITH ICE, POUR THE VODKA AND CHAMBORD LIQUEUR. SHAKE WELL TILL CHILLED AND STRAIN INTO A ROCKS GLASS WITH FRESH ICE. TOP WITH THE CRANBERRY JUICE AND A SPLASH OF GINGER ALE. GARNISH WITH THE MINT SPRIG AND BLACKBERRIES.

WEEK 46

RED, WHITE AND BLUE

1 OZ. GRENADINE
3 OZ. LEMONADE
1 OZ. GREY GOOSE VODKA
1 OZ. DEKUYPER BLUE CURACAO

USING A HIGHBALL GLASS, POUR THE GRENADINE. ADD ICE. USING A COCKTAIL SHAKER FILLED WITH ICE, POUR THE LEMONADE AND VODKA AND SHAKE TILL WELL CHILLED. USING A SPOON, POUR THE LEMONADE/VODKA OVER THE BACK OF THE SPOON, ON TOP OF THE GRENADINE (DO NOT STIR). THEN USING A MEASURING CUP, POUR THE BLUE CURACAO OVER THE BACK OF THE SPOON TO PROVIDE THE FINAL LAYER.

WEEK 47
GOLD RUSH

2 OZ. BOURBON
1 OZ. HONEY SYRUP
¾ OZ. FRESH SQUEEZED LEMON JUICE
LEMON PEEL - GARNISH

USING A COCKTAIL SHAKER WITH ICE, POUR THE BOURBON, HONEY SYRUP AND LEMON JUICE. SHAKE WELL FOR 30 SECONDS, TILL WELL CHILLED. STRAIN INTO A ROCKS GLASS WITH ONE LARGE CUBE. GARNICH WITH A LEMON PEEL.

WEEK 48
JEZEBEL 75

2 STRAWBERRIES
½ OZ. ORANGE JUICE
½ OZ. SIMPLE SYRUP
2 OZ. GREY GOOSE VODKA
KORBEL CHAMPAGNE
HALF STRAWBERRY - GARNISH

USING A COCKTAIL SHAKER, MUDDLE THE STRAWBERRIES, ADDING ORANGE JUICE, SIMPLE SYRUP AND VODKA. ADD ICE AND SHAKE TILL WELL CHILLED. STRAIN INTO A CHILLED COUPE GLASS, TOP WILL CHAMPAGNE AND ADD STRAWBERRY GARNISH.

WEEK 49
EMPRESS LEMONADE

2 OZ. EMPRESS GIN
1 OZ. HONEY SYRUP
2 OZ. LEMONADE
LEMON PEEL - GARNISH

FILL A ROCKS GLASS WITH CRUSHED ICE. USING A COCKTAIL SHAKER, POUR HONEY SYRUP AND LEMONADE OVER ICE AND SHAKE WELL TILL CHILLED. STRAIN INTO ROCKS GLASS OVER ICE. POUR EMPRESS GIN ON TOP, ADDING MORE CRUSHED ICE AND GARNISH WITH LEMON PEEL.

WEEK 50

TEQUILA WALLBANGER

2 OZ. CASAMIGOS TEQUILA BLANCO
½ OZ. GALLIANO
4 OZ. GRAPEFRUIT JUICE
2 DASHES ANGOSTURA ORANGE BITTERS
SAN PELLEGRINO POMPELMO SODA
LIME WEDGE - GARNISH

USING A HIGHBALL GLASS FILLED HALFWAY WITH ICE, ADD TEQUILA, GALLIANO, BITTERS AND GRAPEFRUIT JUICE. STIR AND THEN TOP OFF SAN PELLEGRINO POMPELMO SODA. GARNISH WITH LIME WEDGE.

WEEK 51
AMOR DE FRESA

2 OZ. FOUR ROSES SMALL BATCH SELECT
¼ OZ. SIMPLE SYRUP
3 DASHES ANGOSTURA BITTERS
1 STRAWBERRY
LUXARDO MARASCHINO CHERRY - GARNISH
STRAWBERRY - GARNISH

USING A COCKTAIL SHAKER, ADD STRAWBERRY AND SIMPLE SYRUP AND THEN MUDDLE. ADD BOURBON AND BITTERS AND THEN FILL WITH ICE. STIR TILL WELL CHILLED AND THEN STRAIN INTO A ROCKS GLASS FILLED WITH FRESH ICE. GARNISH WITH THE CHERRY AND STRAWBERRY.

WEEK 52
ADIOS MOTHERFUCKER

½ OZ. CASAMIGOS TEQUILA BLANCO
½ OZ. CAPTAIN MORGAN WHITE RUM
½ OZ. GREY GOOSE VODKA
½ OZ. BOMBAY SAPPHIRE GIN
½ OZ. DEKUYPER BLUE CURACAO
2 OZ. SWEET AND SOUR MIX
7UP
LEMON WEDGE - GARNISH

ADD THE TEQUILA, RUM, VODKA, GIN, BLUE CURACAO AND SWEET AND SOUR MIX TO A HIGHBALL GLASS WITH ICE AND STIR TILL WELL CHILLED. TOP WITH 7UP AND GARNISH WITH LEMON WEDGE.